The social effects of unemployment in Teesside